Oxford Very First Atlas

Editorial Adviser
Dr Patrick Wiegand

OXFORD
UNIVERSITY PRESS

Great Clarendon Street, Oxford OX2 6DP

Oxford University Press is a department of the University of Oxford.
It furthers the University's objective of excellence in research, scholarship,
and education by publishing worldwide in

Oxford   New York

Auckland   Cape Town   Dar es Salaam   Hong Kong   Karachi
Kuala Lumpur   Madrid   Melbourne   Mexico City   Nairobi
New Delhi   Shanghai   Taipei   Toronto

With offices in

Argentina   Austria   Brazil   Chile   Czech Republic   France   Greece
Guatemala   Hungary   Italy   Japan   Poland   Portugal   Singapore
South Korea   Switzerland   Thailand   Turkey   Ukraine   Vietnam

Oxford is a registered trade mark of Oxford University Press
in the UK and in certain other countries

ISBN 978 0 19 848787 6 (hardback)
ISBN 978 0 19 848786 9 (paperback)

7 9 10 8 6

Printed in Singapore by KHL Printing Co. Pte Ltd.

Paper used in the production of this book is a natural, recyclable product
made from wood grown in sustainable forests. The manufacturing process
conforms to the environmental regulations of the country of origin.

TEACHERS
For inspirational support plus
free resources and eBooks
www.oxfordprimary.co.uk

PARENTS
Help your child's reading
with essential tips, fun
activities and free eBooks
www.oxfordowl.co.uk

Acknowledgements

The publishers would like to thank Roderick Hunt for his advice on literacy levels.

The publishers would like to thank the following for permission to reproduce photographs:

Alamy pp 13 (Roger Cracknell), 22 (Visions of America, LLC), 23 (Gary Cook), 25 (Dave Watts),
26 (PeterArnold Inc.), 27 (Steven J. Kazlowski), 29 (John Macpherson); Photolibrary Group pp7 (Radius Images),
21 (Jochen Tack), 32 (Brian Lawrence); Science Photo Library pp 5 (Planetary Visions Ltd), 6 (Planetary Visions
Ltd), 8t (Planetary Visions Ltd), 8b (Planetobserver), 10-11 (Planetobserver), 28 (Planetobserver).
All other photographs supplied by Oxford University Press.

Cover illustrations by Galia Bernstein. Cover globe by Jan Rysavy/iStockphoto.

Contents

Greetings from THE ALPS

Look at pages 18–19.

Having fun in PARIS

Look at pages 18–19.

On holiday in INDIA

Look at pages 20–21.

A postcard from NEW YORK

Look at page 22.

A postcard from EGYPT

Look at page 24.

Greetings from LONDON

Look at page 32.

Can you find these places in the atlas?

4 This is space.

The Earth is a planet in space.

6 The Earth is round, like a ball.

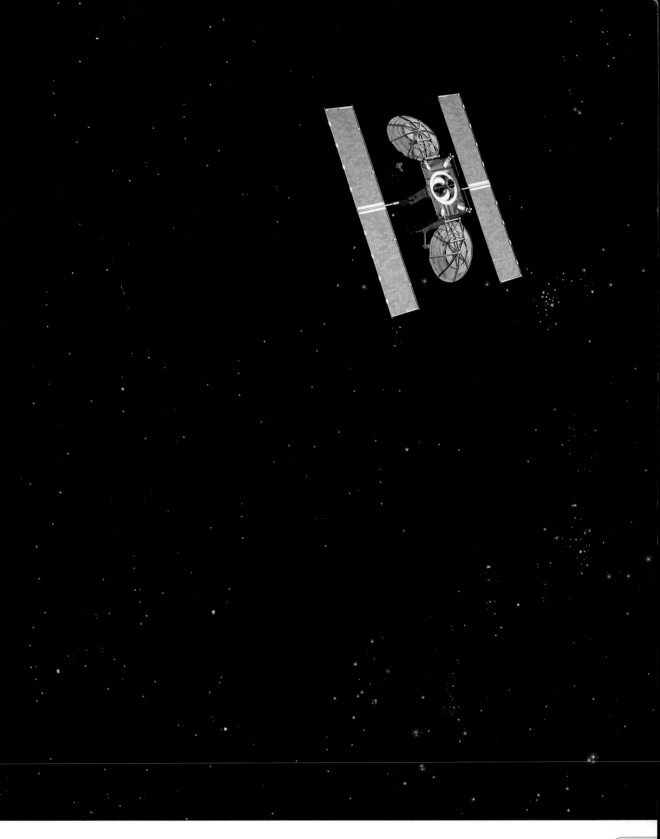

Satellites take pictures of the Earth.

You can see the
whole world.

You can zoom
in close.

These are satellite pictures on a computer.

The Earth has
land and sea.

A globe is a model of the Earth.

10 This is a picture of the Earth from space.

It is laid out flat.

The World

Rocky Mountains

River Mississippi

Atlantic
Ocean

Saha

Pacific
Ocean

River
Amazon

A n d e s

Atlantic
Ocean

Southern Ocean

Key

~~~ river

△ mountains

🌵 desert

This is a map of the world.

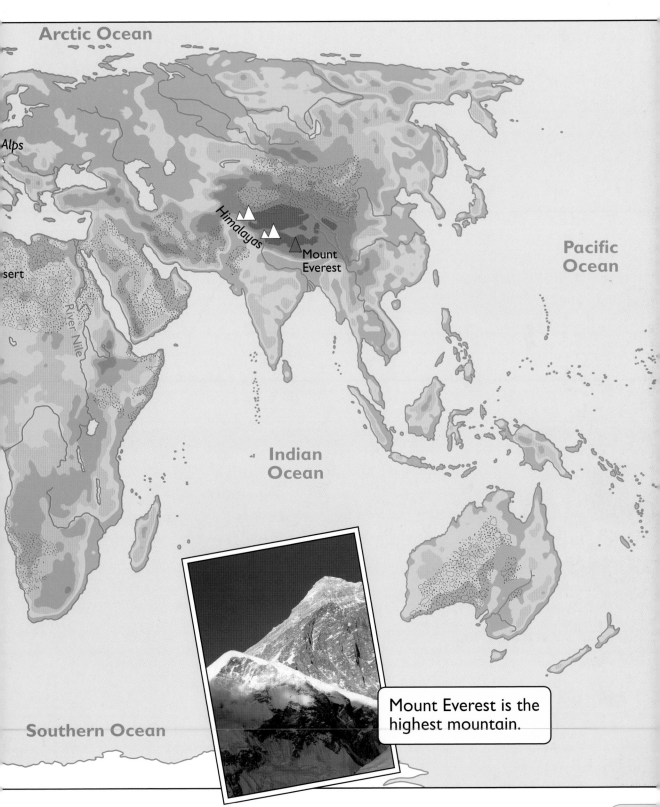

Arctic Ocean

Alps

Himalayas

△ Mount
Everest

Pacific
Ocean

sert

River Nile

Indian
Ocean

Mount Everest is the
highest mountain.

Southern Ocean

It shows rivers, mountains and deserts.

The World

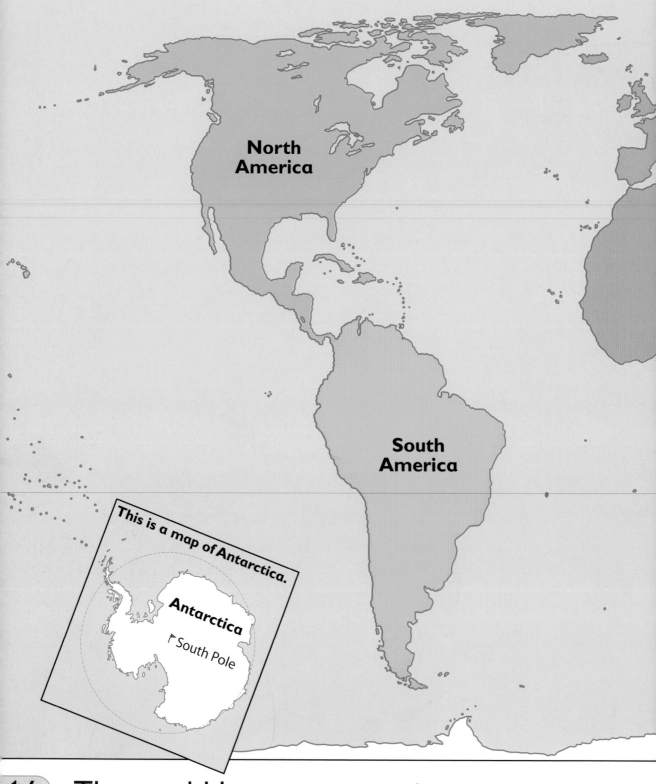

North America

South America

This is a map of Antarctica.

Antarctica

South Pole

The world has seven continents.

Europe

Asia

Africa

Oceania

Antarctica

Continents are very big areas of land.

The World

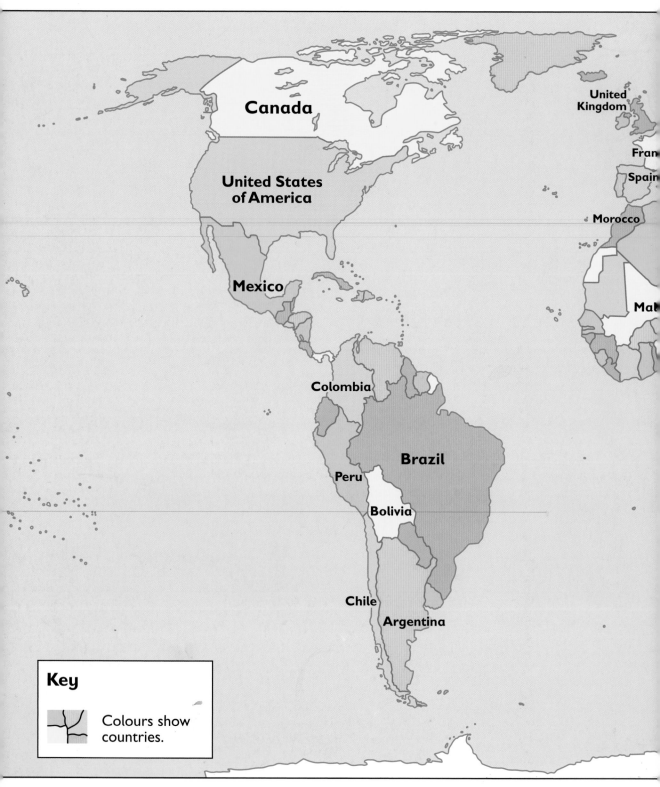

Canada

United Kingdom

Fran[ce]

Spain

United States of America

Morocco

Mexico

Ma[li]

Colombia

Brazil

Peru

Bolivia

Chile

Argentina

Key

Colours show countries.

The world has many countries.

Which country are you from?

Europe

Iceland
- Reykjavik

Sweden

Norway

Oslo ■

Stockholm ■

Denmark

■ Copenhagen

United Kingdom

Republic of Ireland

Dublin ■

London ■

Netherlands

Berlin ■

Poland

Germany

Belgium

Prague ■ **Czech Republic**

Paris ■

River Danube

Vienna ■

Switzerland

Austria

France

△△ △△
A l p s

Italy

■ Rome

Key

Colours show countries.

■ capital cities

river

△ mountains

Madrid ■

Portugal

Spain

Lisbon ■

■ **Malta**

18 Europe is a small continent.

Finland

Helsinki

Tallinn
Estonia

Riga
Latvia

Lithuania
Vilnius

Minsk

Belarus

Warsaw

Kiev

Ukraine

Russia

Moscow

River Volga

Romania

Belgrade

Bucharest

Serbia

Bulgaria

Sofia

Georgia
Tbilisi

Greece

Ankara

Turkey

Athens

Cyprus

Hello   Hola   Buon giorno

God dag   Guten Tag

Bonjour   Yia sas

Dzień dobry   Merhaba

There are many European languages.

Asia

Russia

Moscow

Astana ■

Kazakhstan

Ulan Bator ■

Mongolia

Uzbekistan   Tashkent ■

Gobi Desert

Beijing ■

Turkmenistan
Ashgabat ■

Baghdad   ■ Tehran

Afghanistan   Kabul ■

China

Islamabad ■

Iraq   Iran

Himalayas

Yangtze River

Pakistan

New
Delhi ■

Riyadh ■   Muscat ■

Bangladesh
Dhaka

Hanoi ■

Saudi
Arabia

Oman

Myanmar

Sana ■   Yemen

India

Yangon ■

Thailand
Bangkok ■

Manila ■

Vietnam

Philippines

Malaysia

Kuala Lumpur ■

Jakarta ■   Indonesia

20   Asia is the largest continent.

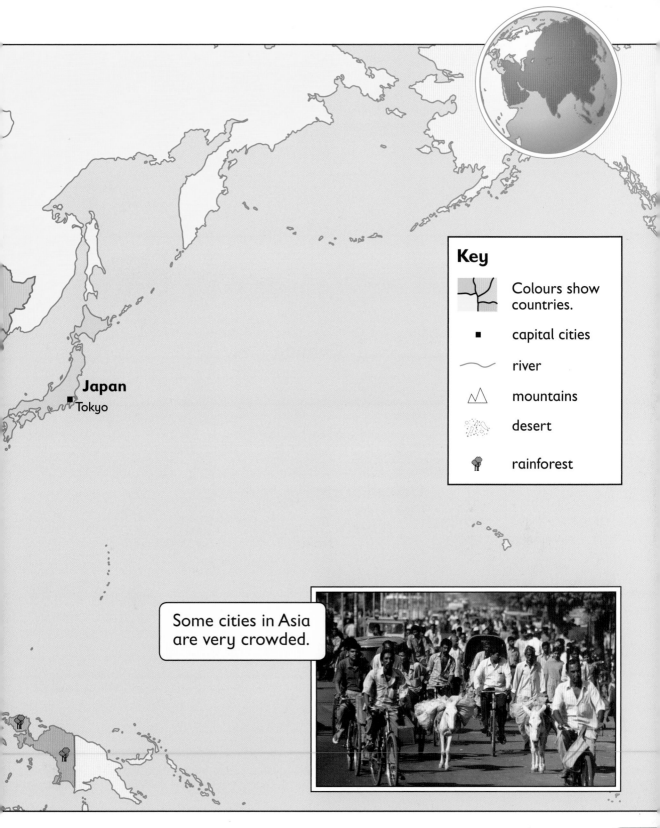

Key

	Colours show countries.
■	capital cities
~	river
△	mountains
⋰	desert
🌳	rainforest

Japan
■ Tokyo

Some cities in Asia are very crowded.

It also has the most people.

North America

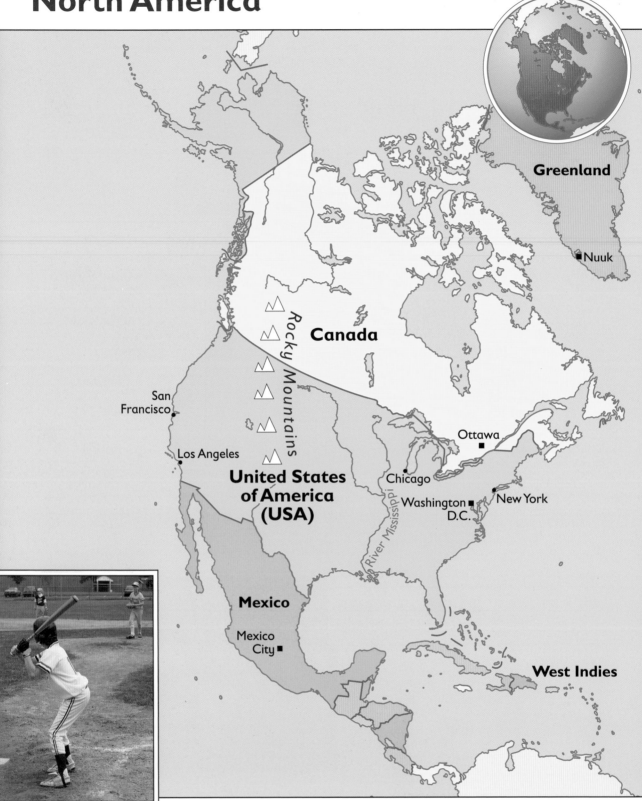

Greenland

Nuuk

Canada

Rocky Mountains

San Francisco

Ottawa

Los Angeles

Chicago

United States of America (USA)

Washington D.C.

New York

River Mississippi

Mexico

Mexico City

West Indies

The USA is the world's richest country.

South America

Caracas

Venezuela

Georgetown Paramaribo
Cayenne

Bogota **Guyana** Suriname **French Guiana**

Colombia

Quito
Ecuador

River Amazon

B r a z i l

Peru

Lima

Bolivia

La Paz

Brasilia

Paraguay

Asuncion

Argentina

Santiago **Uruguay**

Buenos Aires Montevideo

Andes

Chile

Key

Colours show
countries.

■ capital cities

• other cities

～ river

△ mountains

🌳 rainforest

It rains a lot in the
Amazon rainforest.

There is a big rainforest in Brazil.

Africa

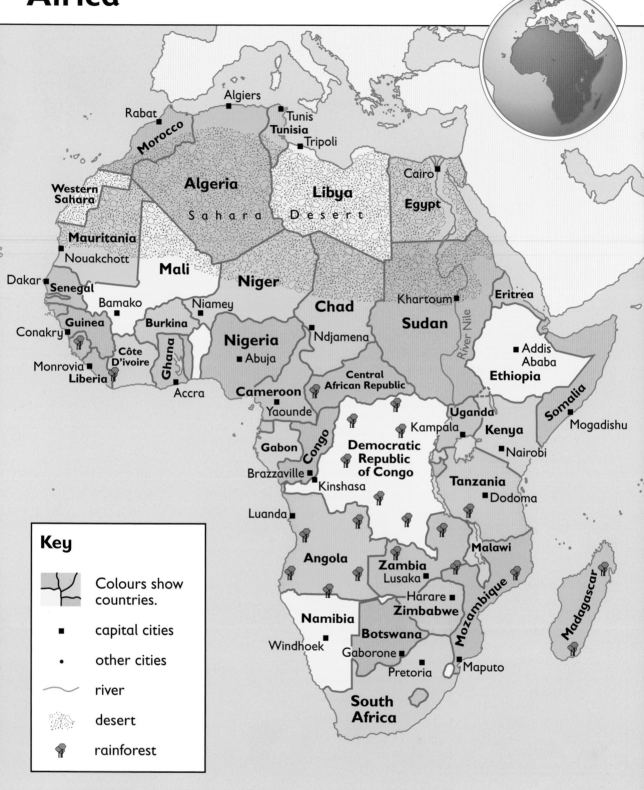

Key

	Colours show countries.
■	capital cities
•	other cities
~	river
	desert
🌳	rainforest

Algiers

Rabat

Tunis
Tunisia

Tripoli

Morocco

Cairo

Western Sahara

Algeria

Libya

Egypt

S a h a r a   D e s e r t

Mauritania

Nouakchott

Mali

Niger

Khartoum

Eritrea

Dakar
Senegal

Bamako

Niamey

Chad

Sudan

Addis Ababa

Conakry
Guinea

Burkina

Ndjamena

River Nile

Ethiopia

Monrovia
Liberia

Côte D'ivoire

Ghana

Nigeria

■ Abuja

Central African Republic

Somalia

Mogadishu

Accra

Cameroon

Yaounde

Uganda

Kampala

Kenya

Nairobi

Gabon

Congo

Democratic Republic of Congo

Brazzaville

Kinshasa

Tanzania

Dodoma

Luanda

Malawi

Angola

Zambia

Lusaka

Mozambique

Madagascar

Harare

Zimbabwe

Namibia

Botswana

Windhoek

Gaborone

Maputo

Pretoria

South Africa

Africa is the hottest continent.

Oceania

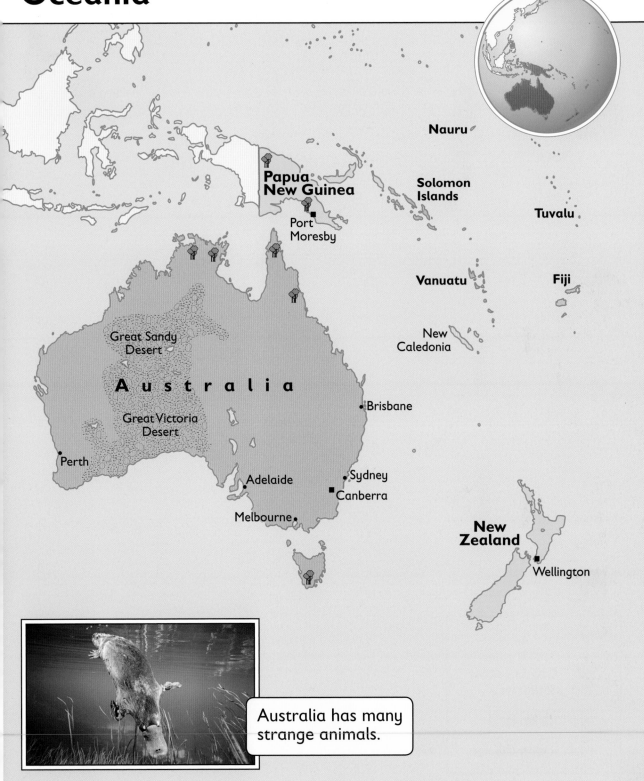

Nauru

Papua
New Guinea

Port
Moresby

Solomon
Islands

Tuvalu

Vanuatu

Fiji

New
Caledonia

Great Sandy
Desert

A u s t r a l i a

Great Victoria
Desert

Brisbane

Perth

Adelaide

Sydney
Canberra

Melbourne

New
Zealand

Wellington

Australia has many
strange animals.

There are lots of islands in Oceania.

Antarctica

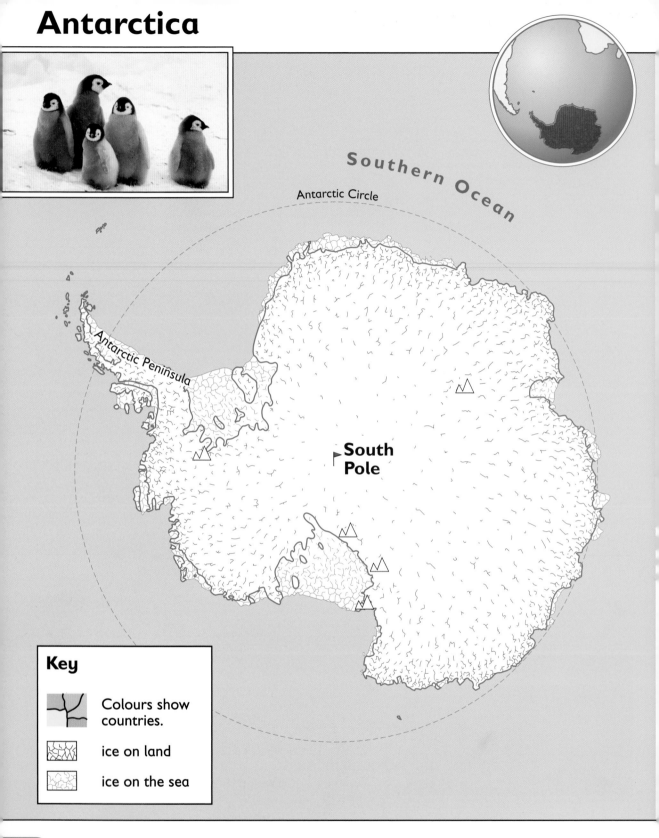

Southern Ocean

Antarctic Circle

Antarctic Peninsula

South
Pole

Key

Colours show
countries.

ice on land

ice on the sea

Antarctica is land covered in ice.

The Arctic Ocean

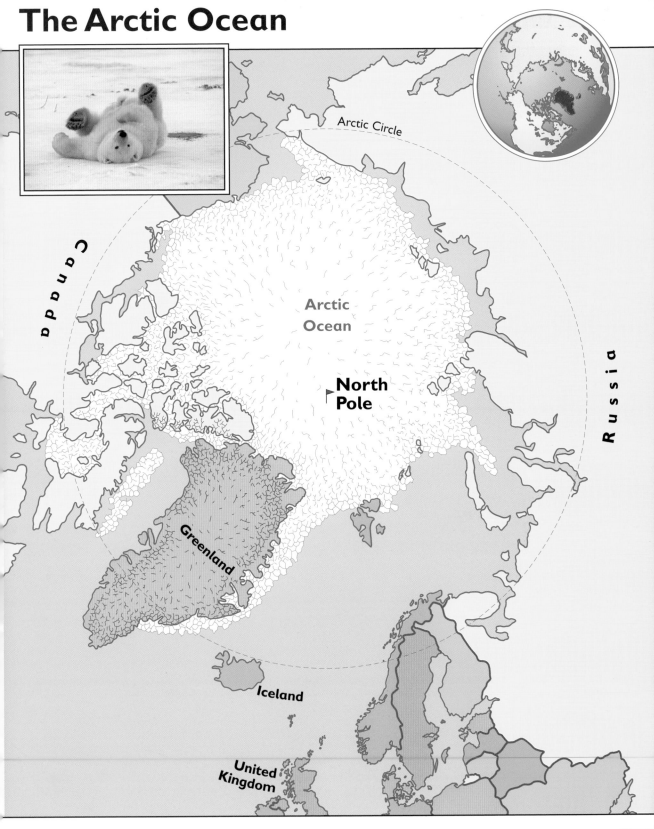

Canada

Arctic Circle

Arctic
Ocean

▶ **North
Pole**

Russia

Greenland

Iceland

United
Kingdom

The Arctic Ocean is frozen water.

The British Isles

This is Great Britain and Ireland from space.

The British Isles

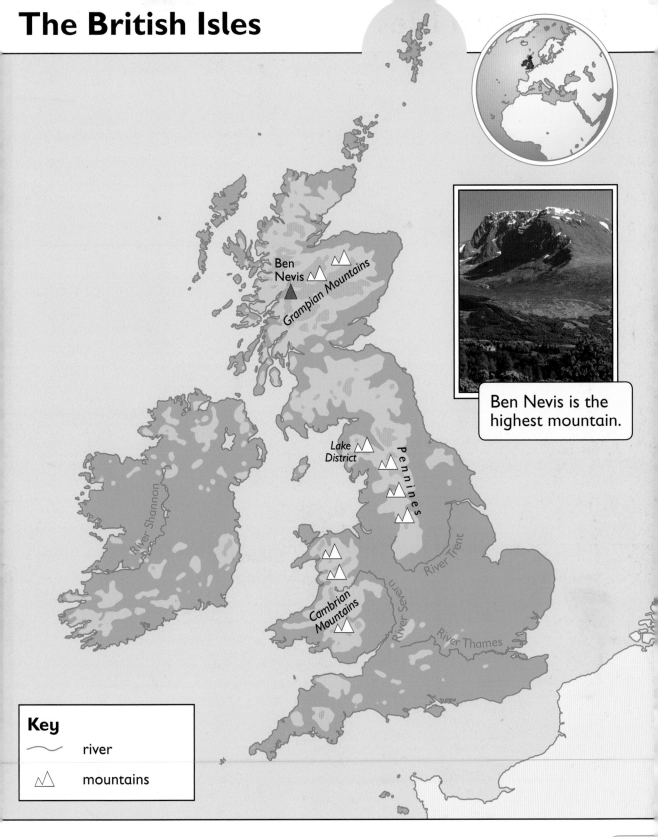

Ben
Nevis

Grampian Mountains

Lake
District

Pennines

Cambrian
Mountains

River Shannon

River Trent

River Severn

River Thames

Ben Nevis is the
highest mountain.

Key

~~~ river

⋀⋀ mountains

This is a map of Great Britain and Ireland.

The British Isles

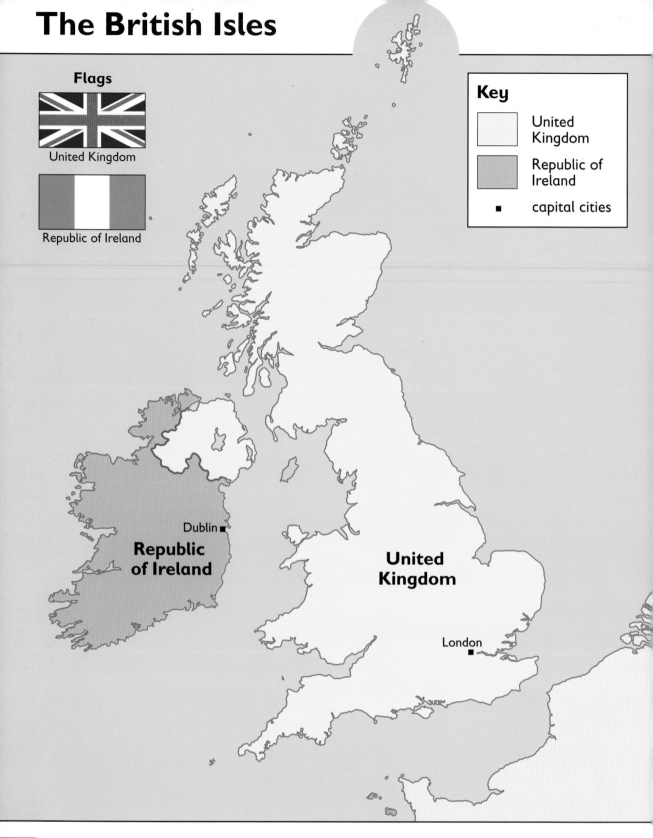

Flags

United Kingdom

Republic of Ireland

Key

United Kingdom

Republic of Ireland

■ capital cities

Dublin ■

Republic of Ireland

United Kingdom

London ■

There are two countries in the British Isles.

The United Kingdom

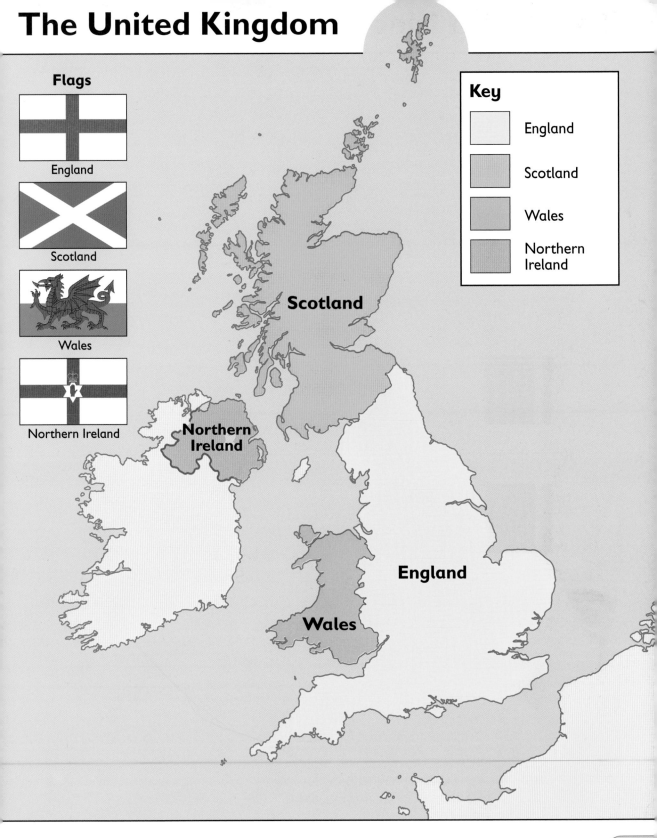

Flags

England

Scotland

Wales

Northern Ireland

Key

England

Scotland

Wales

Northern Ireland

Scotland

Northern Ireland

England

Wales

The United Kingdom has four parts.

The United Kingdom

Key

- ■ capital cities
- 🏛 other big cities
- • other big cities

Scotland

Glasgow ■ Edinburgh

Northern Ireland
Belfast

•Newcastle upon Tyne

Leeds
Manchester
Liverpool •Sheffield
Nottingham

England
Norwich

•Birmingham

Wales
Cardiff
•Bristol   London ■

Southampton

London is the biggest city in the United Kingdom.

There are many big cities.